The Bo Peep
Business Plan

The Bo Peep Business Plan

16 Simple Strategies to Succeed as a Young Entrepreneur

Jane Maulucci

Published by:
Aviva Publishing
Lake Placid, NY 12946
518-523-1320
www.avivapubs.com

AVIVA
PUBLISHING
New York

Every attempt has been made to source all quotes properly.
For additional copies or bulk purchases, please contact:

Susan Friedmann
Aviva Publishing
susan@avivapubs.com

Editor: Beth Cooper Writes, https://www.bethcooperwrites.com
Cover Design: Halpern Designs, https://yael-halpern.my.canva.site/
Interior Layout: Chapter One Book Design, https://chapter-one-book-production.co.uk

Library of Congress Control Number: 2025911663
Paperback ISBN: 978-1-63618-325-1
eBook ISBN: 978-1-63618-326-8

10 9 8 7 6 5 4 3 2 1

First Paperback Edition, 2025

Printed in the United States of America

DEDICATION

To my husband, Seb,
who patiently lives with me and my imagination,
and to Susan and Bonnie for gently shoving me forward.

CONTENTS

FOREWORD
BY MARTIN BROSSMAN

Jane Maulucci was one of those people you don't forget. She lit up every room with her laughter, her curiosity, and her genuine love for helping others. From the moment I met her, I knew she was someone special.

Jane had a gift for turning ideas into something real and meaningful. She believed in small business owners and poured everything she had into supporting them. This book is a perfect example of that. It's creative, practical, and full of her unique spirit.

Even as she faced the toughest challenge of her life, Jane kept working on this project. She wanted it to help people. And now, thanks to the care of her family and friends, it can.

Her words still speak. Her heart is still here. And if this book makes you feel seen or supported, that's Jane—still doing what she loved.

Thank you, Jane. We miss you.

INTRODUCTION

ONCE UPON A TIME...

Fables, fairy tales, and nursery rhymes are designed to help us learn lessons without the pain of a formal lecture. Through the stories and couplets, we learned about honesty and friendship and that animals could talk. We may have overlooked the fact that all the characters in these stories were self-employed.

The butcher, the baker, and the candlestick maker were entrepreneurs utilizing their skills to make a living. Peter Piper sold pickled peppers, Geppetto was a toy maker, and Little Bo Peep was a shepherd. They each had a business with all the usual challenges that business owners face—things like marketing, competition, logistics, and dozing off on the job.

Here are some tales of Little Bo Peep and the other entrepreneurs in her modern community so you might painlessly gain from their experiences and adventures. And, in case you missed out on the original rhymes, fables, and fairy tales, versions of the stories are included for reference in their entirety when possible or interpretively abridged to keep things moving along.

At the end of each chapter, you'll find questions to ponder about your business. It might be helpful to have a notebook handy to record your thoughts and insights so that you can implement your brilliant strategies to make your business more profitable.

Please remember the anecdotes and businesses represented in this book are purely figments of my imagination, and the fictitious characters have been respectfully borrowed from Mother Goose, the Brothers Grimm, and ancient literature.

LITTLE BO PEEP

Little Bo Peep has lost her sheep,
And can't tell where to find them.
Leave them alone, and they'll come home,
Wagging their tails behind them.

Little Bo Peep fell fast asleep,
And dreamt she heard them bleating;
But when she awoke, she found it a joke,
For they were still all fleeting.

Then up she took her little crook,
Determined for to find them;
She found them indeed, but it made her heart bleed,
For they'd left their tails behind them.

It happened one day, as Bo Peep did stray
Into a meadow hard by,
There she espied their tails, side by side,
All hung on a tree to dry.

She heaved a sigh and wiped her eye,
And over the hillocks she raced;
And tried what she could, as a shepherdess should,
That each tail be properly placed.

CHAPTER 1

BO PEEP AND HER SHEEP – BUILDING A BUSINESS PLAN

Some people are born into a business, and little Bo Peep was one of them. Her mom and grandmom, also named Bo Peep, had been shepherds, and so when Peep, as her friends called her, was four years old, she got her first lamb to tend. Her job was to feed it, care for it, and keep track of where it went.

(The tale of Bo Peep losing her sheep was actually about her grandmother, who was known for chasing butterflies while tending her sheep. It only happened once, but you know how families never let you forget!)

Little Bo Peep did so well with that one little lamb that on her next birthday, her mom gave her a starter flock of five sheep to tend.

Peep's sheep joyfully followed her to the meadows in the morning and back home in the afternoon. Their wool sparkled in the sunshine because she fed them only the best clover and freshest water. By the time she was 10, Peep regularly won prizes at the 4-H fairs for her happy herd's soft, thick wool, and her flock was now one hundred sheep.

Days after graduating from high school with honors, Peep talked with the meadow fairy, Miriam, about the possibility of turning her hobby into a business. Miriam took a seat on a daisy and carefully explained why that would be a bad idea. She told Bo Peep that she was too young and too inexperienced and would never be able to run a business and go to college. Miriam explicitly stated that it was silly to try to do something so grand and that Peep should not reach further than her grasp.

Bo Peep respectfully thanked Miriam for her opinion and dejectedly called the sheep in to bring them back home. When she got to the barn, she spotted the barn fairy, Bonnie, playing tag with a dragonfly. Bonnie noticed Bo Peep looked slightly sour and asked about her frowny face. Peep explained that she had an idea to start a business, but Miriam said it wouldn't work.

Bonnie had no tolerance for Mariam's negativity and said, "Of course, you can start a business!"

Bonnie was over the moon at the thought of Bo Peep becoming the best and brightest businessperson ever. She flitted around like a drunken mosquito as she listed all the reasons that Peep would be a success. Now, fully energized and ready to take on the world, Bo Peep headed into the house for dinner.

Peep sat down in the mud room to pull off her mucky boots. Heather, the house fairy, noticed Bo Peep's flush and fire, which could only mean that she was up to something. Heather announced from her perch on the coat rack, "I hope it is good trouble, Bo Peep!"

"Oh, it is!", Peep replied, and all in one breath, she described her business dream and reiterated Bonnie's comments about the expected ease and success she would have making it come true. Heather, always the voice of reason, congratulated Bo Peep for her willingness to start a new venture and followed it with a sincere suggestion to discuss the idea with Peep's mother, who had experience and wisdom that would be very helpful.

With her enthusiasm only slightly tempered, Bo Peep approached her mom and tentatively broached the idea of starting a business. The first question Mom asked was, "Why do you want to start a business?" Bo Peep replied that she really enjoyed working with the sheep and felt she had a talent for keeping them calm, which also helped them produce the most luxurious wool. Bo Peep also saw the business as a way to fund her veterinary education.

Mom was pleased that Bo Peep could easily explain why she wanted the business and what it could do for her. The next steps involved determining the viability of the business and building a business plan. First, she had to identify what her business would be. Would she have a product or a service?

Bo Peep decided that she could have both. Her service would be tending the sheep, which she could do for her own small flock and for other farmers who needed their sheep looked after. The farmers would pay Peep a fee for taking care of their sheep plus a percentage of their sheep's wool each spring. The wool would be the raw material for yarn, her product.

While her idea looked good on paper, Mom encouraged Bo Peep to research if there actually was a market for her business. It could be that the farmers didn't need a shepherd and that the yarn market was already saturated. Bo Peep had to understand if the markets existed and if she could work with them.

Bo Peep started with her service. She talked with the Farmer in the Dell and others about the opportunity to have her tend their flocks. Since many of them were working solo on their farms, she learned that hiring a shepherd, especially one with her reputation, would be beneficial for them.

Then she stopped in at Knit One, the village yarn store, and talked with Tatiana about the types of yarn her customers sought. Bo Peep learned that one product Tatiana wished she offered was an exclusive, high-quality, locally produced yarn that would be especially tantalizing to tourists.

Encouraged by her research, Bo Peep decided to proceed with her business venture and began to build her plan. Before she could determine what to charge for her products and services, Bo Peep had to work out the costs.

Her costs were very detailed, and she created part of her list by mentally walking through a typical day with her sheep and thinking about everything she needed to keep them safe and healthy. Then she added the costs of shearing the sheep, cleaning the wool, spinning the yarn, packing and shipping the yarn, and marketing her service and product.

To get accurate costs, Bo Peep reached out to local suppliers who could provide the services and products she needed. Each of them was willing to give her estimates so that she could build her business plan with accurate numbers rather than uneducated guesses that might be too high or too low. The suppliers wanted to create a positive relationship with Bo Peep even before her business was in full swing so they would be top of mind when she started.

It took considerable time and effort to work out all the details. But now, with her business plan in hand, Bo Peep felt she held a treasure map that would lead her to the success she aimed for.

THINK ABOUT
BUILDING A BUSINESS PLAN

Bo Peep demonstrated that you can start building a business plan with paper and a pencil by asking yourself questions about what you offer and who you serve. Use the questions below to get going on building or refining your business plan.

- What is the product or service that you want to offer?

- What problem do you solve, or what need do you fulfill?

- Who is the ideal customer for your product or service?

- How are you different from your competitors?

- How will you research your market?

- What are the costs associated with your business?

- What resources can you access to build your business plan?

LITTLE BOY BLUE

Little Boy Blue, come blow your horn,
The sheep are in the meadow, the cows in the corn.
Where is the boy who looks after the sheep?
He's under a haystack, fast asleep!

LITTLE MISS MUFFET

Little Miss Muffet sat on a tuffet,
Eating her curds and whey.
Along came a spider
Who sat down beside her,
and frightened Miss Muffet away.

CHAPTER 2

LITTLE BOY BLUE'S BLEAT – BUILDING A BRAND

Little Boy Blue was the town herald. He followed his family tradition of announcing important news and events to the citizens. However, instead of standing in the town square and blowing his bugle to assemble the townsfolk as his predecessors had, he used digital methods such as social media and podcasts to alert the masses to the local news, from births and birthdays to lost pets and daily luncheon specials.

In his spare time, which seemed endless, he was a prankster and loved to startle his unsuspecting victim with a bleat from his bugle. Most people took it pretty well. However, Miss Muffet was not one to trifle with, especially after her arachnid adventure (she hated spiders and surprises), and she put a dent in Blue's bugle bell to confirm her displeasure.

One day, as Bo Peep sat under her favorite tree, tending her flock and studying organic chemistry, Little Boy Blue attempted to sneak up on her sheep and startle them. He had been planning it all day and inched his way into the field so quietly that even Sheba, Bo Peep's sheepdog, hadn't heard him approach.

He was mere inches from the flock when he pulled out his bugle and blasted a loud "TAAA-DAAA!"

The sheep didn't even flinch. Sheba, just lifted her head and gave him a look of disdain. Bo Peep laughed so hard as she trotted down the hill that she almost tripped. "Tried to scare my sheep, did you?", she chuckled. Little Boy Blue was red in the face; his prank didn't go as planned. He couldn't understand why those sheep just ignored his ear-shattering bugle bleat.

Bo Peep told him that her sheep were always relaxed and never even bothered by thunderstorms. Then she announced, "You've been a great help! I needed to think of a name for the yarn I'll be selling, and now I've got it: Calm Lamb!"

Boy Blue was confused and couldn't comprehend why she required a unique name for her yarn. Bo Peep explained that it was more than a name. She wanted a brand that would be distinctive and memorable for people looking for her yarn.

She had considered putting her name on the yarn but decided to give it a separate identity. She had wanted a name that would attract buyers and make them think of her yarn first above all other choices. *Calm Lamb* fit the bill as it gave the feeling that something made from this wool would be soothing and comfortable.

Then Bo Peep sketched a picture of a happy little lamb lying on the grass to use as her logo, an eye-catching way to distinguish it from other brands. The colors she chose were deep purple and warm cream. The purple represented luxury, and the cream was for the calm, relaxed lamb.

Next, she created a tagline succinctly describing her yarn to attract people who knit and crochet and get them excited about using her product. Bo Peep knew that needleworkers often make gifts for other people, and they feel good creating a scarf, sweater, or blanket to keep their loved ones warm. With that in mind, she came up with "Warming Hearts & Hands."

Now, she was ready to have the graphic artist at the print shop design her labels, business cards, signage, and other collateral she would use to promote and sell her yarn. She would put the logo (the lamb) and her tagline (Warming Hearts & Hands) on everything associated with the yarn to make a consistent and constant connection to her particular product.

She thanked Little Boy Blue for the inspiration. Even though that was not at all his plan, he happily accepted her gratitude and started plotting his next prank.

THINK ABOUT
BUILDING A BRAND

Your brand helps people connect with who you are and what you do. It requires you to think about your solution and who it best serves. Once you've identified your brand logo, colors, and tagline you can use your branding to quickly connect with the people who need what you offer.

- What makes your product or service unique?

- What emotion do you want your brand to generate?

- What is your brand personality?

- What is the story behind your brand?

- What colors represent your brand?

- What does your logo say about your brand?

- How are you using your branding consistently?

RUMPLESTILTSKIN

A poor miller had a beautiful daughter named Rachel. One day, he bragged about her spinning skills, as she was talented at turning wool, linen, and hemp into lovely threads and yarns. "Why she can spin straw into gold," he boasted. The boast was repeated to the greedy king, and at once, he had the miller's daughter brought to the palace and put in a tiny dark cell piled with straw and a spinning wheel.

The king said, "Turn this straw into gold by daybreak, and you shall have your choice of any of my sons for your husband. If you are unsuccessful, then you shall be hanged." As it was, Rachel and the king's youngest son, Erwin, were secretly engaged, so aside from saving her own life, she decided to give it a go.

Try as she might, she soon found that straw would not turn into gold and started weeping. "Stop your crying!" a gruff voice said. It belonged to a scruffy little man who had climbed in through the bars on the window. "I can turn that straw into gold, but I need payment." Rachel offered her necklace, and the odd creature quickly spun beautiful gold thread from the straw. Then he slipped back out through the window.

The following day, the king arrived and was thrilled with her skill. Rather than let her leave, he brought in twice as much straw for her to spin by the next morning. When he left, she again began to cry, and the odd little man appeared. "I will spin for you, but you must pay me!" he snarled. She reluctantly offered him her ring, a gift from Erwin. He accepted it, spun the straw, and dashed out the window.

The sun rose, and the King appeared at the doorway, gleeful at the room filled with gold thread. This time, he escorted Rachel out of the tiny cell and moved her to the one next to it that was twice as large and filled to the ceiling with straw. The King promised that this would be her last task, and if she were successful, she would finally be released. When the door closed, Rachel couldn't help but start to wail and cry, which seemed to be her only way to summon the cranky little man.

He arrived and demanded payment before he started spinning. Rachel explained that she had nothing left to give, so the grump bargained to take her firstborn in exchange for his skill. She quickly agreed, fully expecting that he would never come to collect. As before, he spun the straw into gold and exited through the window.

A year later, Rachel was holding her firstborn child when the ornery creature strutted into the castle to demand his payment. Rachel would not surrender the child and begged to renegotiate their bargain. The imp agreed that she could keep the child if she could guess his name within three days. Now a princess, Rachel reluctantly agreed, and after he left, she sent messengers all across the country to learn his name.

The first day he returned, she said, "Is it Caspar, Melchior, Balthazar...?"

"NO! That is not my name!" said the homely spinner.

The next day, she tried running through the alphabet and making up crazy names like Roastribs and Spindleshanks. Still no luck; she did not know his name. She only had one more day to learn his name and keep her child.

That evening, a messenger arrived and told Rachel he had seen a funny little man singing in a growly voice and dancing around a campfire. The spy reported that at the end of his song, he said, "... and my name is RUMPLESTILTSKIN!"

At dawn, the scruffy man appeared; Rachel was cool and confident. She welcomed him with a smile and said, "What a pleasure to see you, RUMPLESTILTSKIN!" And he disappeared in a puff of smoke.

CHAPTER 3

SPINNING GOLD – MENTORSHIP

Bo Peep was so excited about the new branding that she rushed straight into town to tell Tatiana, the owner of *Knit One*. A few months earlier, Bo Peep had arranged to have her wool turned into yarn, packaged, and sold through Tatiana's store.

Tatiana gushed with compliments when she saw the logo, colors, and tagline, and she also felt anxious. She knew that having the branding meant Bo Peep was ready to start processing and selling her yarn. However, the woman who had spun yarn for *Knit One* recently and unexpectedly retired, and, unfortunately, Tatiana didn't know how to spin wool! Since she didn't want to ruin Bo Peep's excitement or cause her any worry, she kept that secret to herself.

After Bo Peep left the store, Tatiana quickly called her sister-in-law Rachel at *Rumple Mills* and explained her predicament. She knew Rachel had the people and the expertise to help her.

Rachel's great-great-grandfather had established *Rumple Mills* and was the inspiration for the story Rumpelstiltskin. His real name was Sam Rumple. In his time, he turned hemp fiber into all sorts of thread and yarn to make clothing, linens, and even rope, for which he was well paid but not necessarily in gold. Rather than grumpy, he had been a very happy guy with a lovely wife, Anna, and five children, whose heirs now kept the family business buzzing.

At first, Rachel suggested that the mill could spin it for her, but Tatiana said that wouldn't work because Bo Peep had explicitly asked for hand spinning to produce her high-end exclusive yarn. Then Rachel offered to teach Tatiana how to spin the wool since the spinning wheel was already at the store and Tatiana had time after hours to do the work. Tatiana quickly agreed to accept Rachel's help but knew there would be a cost. (It was in the Rumple genes to strike a bargain.)

Tatiana was right! In return, Rachel requested that *Knit One* feature a storefront display of the Rumple Mill products for their upcoming 200th anniversary in September. Tatiana readily consented and started learning to spin that very evening.

Under Rachel's guidance, it took Tatiana a few weeks to efficiently master turning the fleece into yarn. By the time Bo Peep was ready to bring in her wool, Tatiana was a confident spinner and knew she could handle the project. And when fall arrived, the *Knit One* shop window looked especially festive with the Rumple Mills 200th Anniversary display.

THINK ABOUT
MENTORSHIP

There is likely something you would like to learn more about so that you are a better businessperson and have a more profitable business. It is also likely that someone in your business community is willing to mentor you to improve or expand your skills. Use these questions to identify what you'd like to learn and who may be a mentor for you. And remember to return the favor!

- What skills would you like to learn or improve through mentorship?

- Who are the business leaders in your community?

- Who do you know that could mentor you in your business?

- What business questions do you have for your mentor?

- What skills and knowledge would you be willing to share?

STONE SOUP

Many years ago, somewhere very far away, three hungry and weary minstrels were walking through a village on their way home. They had just a bit of water and some dry bread, which did not make a very nourishing meal.

The villagers had heard that strangers were coming and promptly hid all their food, put their kids, dogs, and cats inside the house, and locked all their doors and windows. When the minstrels arrived, the village looked deserted, except for the one house where Mayor Jones lived. The minstrels could see him peeking out from behind a curtain.

Peter bellowed to Paul and Mary so the whole village could hear, "Oh, we are so hungry. If only there were people here who would share just a tiny bit of their larder, we could repay them with music."

Suddenly, Mary spotted a large kettle. She announced in her loudest voice, "Let's take this kettle to the village green, fill it with water, and make our famous Stone Soup!" The other two agreed, and with great dramatic flourishes, singing and acting as if they were on stage, Paul started the fire, Mary found three large rocks, and Peter fetched the water. Soon, the kettle was bubbling, and more people were peeking out at the strangers and wondering about their stone soup.

Vanya, the village busybody, got up her courage, left her

*home, and walked up to the kettle. "That's not much of a soup,"
she told the minstrels. "You need some potatoes and carrots for
a good soup." And then she went to get some from her house.*

*On her way home, Mayor Jones beckoned from his front
door for a report about the strangers and their stone soup.
After hearing about the meager ingredients, he decided to
contribute, too and brought out some onions and spices. Not to
be outdone, Smitty, who lived next door, went to his garden and
picked spinach and tomatoes to add to the pot.*

*Soon, the entire village had contributed something to the
stone soup. As it simmered and the aroma wafted around the
green, people chatted with the minstrels, and more villagers
came out to set up tables and chairs, plates and silverware,
and bread and butter so everyone could enjoy the meal.*

*By dinnertime, the stone soup was ready, and all the
villagers were on the green, eager to celebrate their visitors
and share the bounty. And, as promised, the minstrels played
and sang well into the evening and were offered the best beds
to rest in before continuing their journey the next day.*

CHAPTER 4

STONE SOUP – BUYING LOCAL

Uncle Lou was in his 90s when he realized that running his cozy café, *Stone Soup*, was getting to be a little much for him. So he asked his nephews, Ross and John, who were living in London, to return to town and run the restaurant. They were thrilled to jump into taking over the family business.

Since Ross was an excellent chef, he would manage the kitchen, and John loved making people feel welcome, so he would run the front of the house and take care of the book-keeping. Both agreed with Uncle Lou to continue his tradition of using local farmers and businesses to supply the restaurant whenever possible.

That was until John found out that the table linens they were getting from *Rumple Mills* were more expensive than the ones he could buy online. He didn't think Uncle Lou would notice the change, so he ordered the online napkins and tablecloths.

Meanwhile, Ross learned that the vast warehouse store 40 miles away sold fruit and vegetables at much-reduced prices. Again, he didn't think Uncle Lou would see the difference and thought his uncle would appreciate the cost savings, so Ross ordered his supplies and planned to make the trek to pick them up.

The linens arrived early one morning, and John was ready to set the 12 bistro tables. Unfortunately, when he opened the packages, he found that the tablecloths and napkins were terribly wrinkled! Somehow, he had to iron all 144 napkins and 24 tablecloths before the lunch crowd came in.

Uncle Lou discovered John in the back room, having little success pressing out the wrinkles with a steam iron. "Those look terrible," said Uncle Lou, "I can't believe *Rumple Mills* would send you such messy linens!" Sheepishly, John confessed that he had not used the local resource but had chosen an online vendor instead, and he apologized for not trusting his uncle's judgment. Uncle Lou quickly called the mill, and the correct wrinkle-free linens arrived just in time for John to get the tables set for lunch.

Meanwhile, Ross was in the kitchen shaking his head. He had planned to serve strawberry shortcake for the dessert special, and all the strawberries from the warehouse store were not as red and delicious as the local ones. Again, Uncle Lou stepped in and called the *Farmer in the Dell*, who delivered juicy, deep-red strawberries to the kitchen in minutes. Ross was embarrassed and grateful that Uncle Lou was willing to forgive him.

After the lunch rush, Uncle Lou sat down with Ross and John and did what he should have done earlier, explained why he shopped locally. He said, "First of all, I know their products are excellent. Secondly, I know the people and that they will back up their products. And third, we all live in the same community, and we support each other and our community when we shop locally."

Uncle Lou went on to say that there are times when he couldn't get something local, so he had to go out of town or online. But first, he always looked to the people he knows, likes, and trusts to see if they can solve his problem and fill his needs.

From then on, John and Ross followed their uncle's advice and built strong relationships with the farmers and vendors in their little town, and they were all successful together.

THINK ABOUT
BUYING LOCAL

Buying locally is a choice we can make every day. When small businesses get to know each other and support each other through their purchases and recommendations, everybody wins. Use these questions to understand how you can and do support your local small businesses.

- What are some of the local businesses that you depend on?

- Which local businesses and organizations do you recommend?

- How can you tap into local businesses more regularly?

PETER PIPER

Peter Piper picked a peck of pickled peppers.
A peck of pickled peppers Peter Piper picked.
If Peter Piper picked a peck of pickled peppers,
How many pickled peppers did Peter Piper pick?

CHAPTER 5

PETER PIPER'S PICKLED PEPPER PREDICAMENT – INVOICING

When Peter Piper retired from the Bremen Town Musicians, he used part of his savings to buy a small organic farm and began growing a variety of peppers ranging from sweet to scorching hot.

Peter had known John and Ross since they were kids and had remained in touch over the years. So, he was thrilled when they took over their uncle's restaurant and thought they might enjoy his pickled peppers. Sure enough, they did, and they offered to feature *Peter Piper's Pickled Peppers* daily on the *Stone Soup* menu.

Peter set a price for each jar and started his friends with one case of 12. By the end of the month, *Stone Soup* was ordering 6 cases! That was great for Peter, but he had one problem. Since John and Ross were such good friends, he didn't know how to ask them to pay for the pickled peppers.

He decided the solution to the problem was not to deliver any more cases until they paid for the first ones. Peter figured they would soon realize they needed to pay him when they missed the peppers.

Ross did notice that he was running out of Peter's peppers and asked John to get more. But, when John called, Peter was too embarrassed to answer his phone and ask his friends to pay their bills.

John sent a text and an email to follow up with the phone call, but Peter still wouldn't reply. He avoided Ross and John, so he didn't have to be uncomfortable asking them to pay what they owed him.

A few days later, Peter was walking down Main Street and bumped into John coming out of *Knit One*. "Peter! I have been trying to reach you! We need more of your pickled peppers. We have been using them in our recipes, and we want to set up a special display so people can buy a jar to take home. Why haven't you responded?"

Peter blushed and mumbled softly, "You haven't paid me for the cases I've already delivered." John gasped! "I pay all our vendors monthly, just like Uncle Lou did. Do I have your invoice? Did you send me the bill?"

Peter fumbled for words, "No, I thought that since we are buddies, we had set a price, and you knew how many cases you had gotten, that you would just send the payment." John smiled and understood that being in business was new for Peter, so he gently clarified that you, as the vendor, **always** send a bill.

That way, the customer and merchant know what has been sold and what needs to be paid. "I have many different vendors," John said, "And I can't keep track of them in my head. Ross and I have been so worried about you. Your pickles are a hit! We can sell more!"

Peter immediately returned to his office to set up a billing system to invoice *Stone Soup* and all his other customers every month without fail or embarrassment. And every last one of them happily paid their bills on time.

THINK ABOUT
INVOICING

If you have ever hesitated to bill a client or just overlooked your billing for a month or two, you are not alone. And if you are consistently up to date on all invoicing, you have a lot of company, too. Use these questions to assess how you handle your invoices and where you might be able to improve.

- How did you establish your product price list or your fees for services?

- How do you get your customer/client to commit to paying you?

- When do you do your invoicing?

- What system do you use for your invoicing?

- How do you handle overdue invoices?

- How can you improve your invoicing system?

THINK ABOUT
PARTNERSHIP

BONUS! Peter Piper partnered with Stone Soup to sell his pickled peppers. Think about your partnership opportunities. They should be businesses that serve the same market such as a veterinarian and a doggy day care.

- Which local businesses could you partner with?

JACK SPRAT

Jack Sprat could eat no fat;
His wife could eat no lean.
And so, between them both,
They licked the platter clean.

CHAPTER 6

THE SPRATS – TEAMWORK

Jack and Joanna Sprat were very different people, and not just in what they ate. Jack was vegan and consumed no animal products. Joanna followed a high-protein diet and ate lots of fish, poultry, and tofu. They'd met in a college biology class and became friends when they were on the track team. He ran cross country and marathons while she was a sprinter and the closer on the women's 4 x 100 relay team. These sports were perfectly suited to their personalities.

Jack liked having a long-term plan and taking each small step to ensure it was done correctly and on schedule. Joanna was a quick problem solver with a daily to-do list that had to be completed before she headed home for the day.

A few years after college, they married and opened their gym together. Because of their different interests and attitudes, they identified which areas of the business each one would lead. Jack jumped in and built their long-term business plan for 1, 3, and 5 years. Joanna took charge of the daily accounting, including ordering supplies and keeping track of memberships. Both were responsible for training sessions; Joanna led the aerobics classes, and Jack focused on weight training.

At the end of each business week, Joanna created a report that gave a snapshot of the business and its finances. Then, together, she and Jack would review the information and determine what adjustments they must make and who would take the lead on a new project, like marketing or community involvement.

One day, a member asked when a pool would be added to the gym, and Jack, thinking it was a great idea, said, "Oh, in about six months!" Joanna overheard his comment, and though she was not thrilled, she smiled and reminded herself to speak to him after the gym closed for the day.

When they finished wiping down the equipment, sweeping and mopping the floors, and emptying the trash, Joanna asked Jack about the pool. His eyes widened, and he spluttered, "It's a really good idea! Think of how that would increase membership and the services we offer."

Joanna agreed it was a good idea, but the timing was off. First, the two of them hadn't talked about it. Second, they needed to review their plan to see if it would support their goals. And third, they had to be sure they could afford to make the investment.

The next day, Jack saw the member who had asked about the pool and explained that he had misspoken. He meant to say that he and Joanna were reviewing the possibility and would have a decision in about six months.

Joanna also overheard that conversation, and this time, her smile was sincere because she knew that she and Jack were on the same team working toward the same goals.

THINK ABOUT
TEAMWORK

Unlike the Sprats, you may not have an actual partner in your business, but you do have team members. Solo or not, you have colleagues, contractors, and systems that help you run your business. Plus, you can build a team of collaborators, advisors, and like-minded business professionals who can serve as a sounding board and a resource for information, inspiration, and support.

Use these questions to consider all the people and organizations that help you run your business.

- Who is on your team?

- How do you split your business responsibilities?

- How do you make decisions for your business?

- Who do you go to for advice and guidance on your business?

RAPUNZEL

Rapunzel was a beautiful child who was orphaned when she was 12. She was immediately adopted by her neighbor, a witch, who may have had something to do with the disappearance of Rapunzel's parents (and the sudden appearance of a pair of cardinals that stayed close to Rapunzel). To protect the child from the dangers of the world until she was an adult, the witch shut Rapunzel up in a thirty-foot tall ivory tower. The imposing tower had windows facing each direction so Rapunzel could see the world, but deadly thorns and briers surrounded it to discourage any visitors.

No one knew that Rapunzel was in the tower except the witch, who visited her every day at noon. The witch was so scary that even the briers would cower away to give her a clear path to the base of the tower. Then she would call out, "Rapunzel, Rapunzel, let down your long hair!" Rapunzel would comply, and the witch would climb the tresses as if they were a rope.

These visits continued for many years, and Rapunzel grew bored with her solitary visitor. One day, the Prince was heading back through the forest to the palace when he heard the witch make her daily request. Concealed by the thick pine trees nearby, he watched as Rapunzel's alternative rope, golden hair, dropped from the tower and the witch scaled it to the entry.

The prince stayed hidden until the witch left the same way she had arrived. As evening approached, the Prince started to make his way to the tower. When he approached the briers, he pulled out his sword to hack his way through, but at the sight of the blade, the plants just moved aside rather than be cut to shreds. Finally, at the tower's base, he called out, "Rapunzel, Rapunzel, let down your long hair!" Rapunzel complied and was startled to see someone other than the witch appear at her window!

The Prince introduced himself and asked how long Rapunzel had been trapped in the tower. She replied, "Over six years, and it is time for me to go! Do you have a horse?" The Prince said he did. Rapunzel quickly braided her hair, snatched the Prince's sword to hack it off, used his dagger to pin it to the window casing, and was on the ground before the Prince could say, "Where to?"

They hopped on his horse and headed to the castle as the cardinals fluttered behind. And, with the help of the Queen, Rapunzel was protected and free to do what she liked.

CHAPTER 7

RAPUNZEL THE INTROVERT WRITER – TIME MANAGEMENT

Bo Peep's friend Rapunzel wasn't really locked in her tower by an evil sorceress. She was a writer, and the only way she could have a quiet place to work was to go to her reclusive tower. She did have extremely long hair, but thanks to her writing success she had installed a private elevator to access her office rather than using her tresses.

One thing Rapunzel was keen on was managing her deadlines. She wrote for the local newspaper and two online magazines, had a blog, edited books, and created website content. She needed a good time management system to keep all those assignments straight.

The first thing she did was establish consistent office hours. She began her day at 7:00 a.m. to have at least two hours of quiet before her clients started calling. The early start also allowed her time to work on her vanity project – a musical comedy about a writer and their pet rabbit.

Then, at 9:00, she would review her emails and respond to any that needed her attention. By 9:30, she checked her daily plan to determine what she would work on first. Usually, she chose the most challenging project to get started on, which enabled her to stop dreading it and break it down into smaller, more manageable pieces.

By 11:00, she was ready for a break and did some yoga stretches to rev up her brain. Then, she'd return any calls or texts she had received and confirm that she was on track with her deadlines. If it were up to her, she'd skip lunch, but she found that it was a necessary break, so she scheduled it into her calendar for 12:30 every afternoon.

After lunch, she would peek at her emails to see if anything needed her immediate attention and then spend the rest of the afternoon productively checking off the deadlines on her daily plan. Finally, around 4:30, she used the last 15 to 30 minutes of her day to confirm her schedule for the following day.

She carved out specific times she would leave open for business meetings: Wednesdays from 10:00 a.m. until noon and Tuesdays and Thursdays from 2:00–4:00 p.m. Of course, she preferred to meet by video chat best of all, but on occasion, she would allow certain clients to enter her ivory tower, and only by appointment. (She was very tidy and didn't want anything to be out of place when they arrived.)

By guarding her time and respecting her client's needs, she was productive, prompt, and profitable.

THINK ABOUT
TIME MANAGEMENT

Not all of us work 9:00 a.m. to 5:00 p.m. Some of us have the luxury (or curse) of working at what others would consider odd hours, like early morning or late at night. Whatever your schedule, having a plan will make you more productive and efficient. Use these questions to start refining your time management.

- How do you feel about how you manage your time?

- What does your ideal workday look like?

- When and how do you prioritize your tasks?

- What are your distractions, and how could you control them?

- Who or what could help you better manage your time?

THE THREE LITTLE PIGS

The three little pigs each built their own home: one of straw, one of sticks, and one of bricks. Each pig thought his house was the best and took great pride in it. Life was lovely except for their neighbor, the Big Bad Wolf. He had a hankering for pork and was threatening to eat them.

A perfectly beautiful sunny day was ruined by the wolf's arrival. He came storming into the neighborhood and stopped at the straw house. He stuck his face in the window and saw one little pig sitting at his kitchen table sipping tea. The Wolf bellowed, "Little Pig, Little Pig, let me come in!"

The pig jumped up, spilling his tea, and squealed, "Not by the hair on my chinny, chin, chin!"

The wolf was not happy, "Then I'll huff, and I'll puff, and I'll blow your house in!" The little pig ran out the back door to his brother's stick house while the wolf huffed, puffed, and turned his home into a haystack.

The wolf moved on to the stick house, where the two little pigs were trying to gather their wits and call the authorities for help. The wolf hollered, "Little Pigs, Little Pigs, let me come in!"

The pigs hugged each other, dropped the phone, and squealed, "Not by the hairs on our chinny, chin, chins!"

The wolf was getting angry and said, "Then I'll huff, and

I'll puff, and I'll blow your house in!" The little pigs jumped out the back window and ran to their brother's brick house while the wolf huffed, puffed, and turned the stick house into kindling.

Now very frustrated, the wolf moved on to the brick house, where the three little pigs were determined to stand their ground. The wolf hollered, "Little Pigs, Little Pigs, let me come in!"

The three pigs defiantly stomped their feet and yelled, "Not by the hairs on our chinny, chin, chins!"

The wolf was enraged yelling, "Then I'll huff, and I'll puff, and I'll blow your house in!" The little pigs stood in the living room armed with the fireplace poker while the wolf huffed and puffed until he could huff and puff no more. Exhausted, the wolf skulked away and stopped by the grocery store for a rotisserie chicken.

The three little pigs celebrated their triumph with a spinach salad, no bacon.

CHAPTER 8

THE NOT SO BIG BAD WOLF – REPUTATION MANAGEMENT

Butch Wolf decided to become an expert in social media and reputation management after he witnessed the damage his dad, Billy, experienced when doing nothing more than his job.

Billy Wolf was the village building inspector, and on a sunny afternoon, he traveled to the site of three newly constructed homes built with innovative materials by the sons of the renowned Pigg Brothers Builders.

The elder Pigg Brothers had established a reputation for sturdy construction at a good value. Their sons wanted to try new techniques and materials, which the elders monitored so that their reputation remained unblemished.

Billy was known as a rule follower. He knew the building codes inside and out and was very thorough in his inspections. The Pigg Brothers, his contemporaries, took it as a point of pride when they passed a Billy Wolf inspection. However, the little Piggs saw Billy Wolf as a chain-smoking, grumpy old guy who should be retired, even though he was barely 50. To be fair, Billy smoked constantly, hardly got any exercise, had a lousy diet, and tended to be short-tempered, especially when challenged, and he looked worn out.

At the first house, Billy took a drag from his ever-present cigarette and started coughing and flailing around, dismantling the house made of straw. The younger Piggs were furious and screamed at him, accusing him of intentionally demolishing it. One of them pulled out his phone and began recording the incident. Billy, still hacking and getting angrier as he tried to defend himself, stumbled into the stick house, and it collapsed.

With two test houses destroyed and video to show the incident, Pigg Brother Builders contacted the press, posted the debacle on their website, and even went live on social media to say that it was Billy's fault that the buildings collapsed. They were trying to protect their stellar reputation by putting the blame on Billy. But, of course, they never mentioned that the three little Piggs had used poor-quality experimental building materials. (The brick house was just fine, so keep that in mind for your next construction project.)

Things got rough for Billy. He managed to keep his job because he was very good at it. However, all the townspeople who had seen the video started to believe the demolition was his fault and nicknamed him the Big Bad Wolf.

It was so bad that his wife, Brenda, stepped in and decided it was time to make some changes. She convinced Billy to quit smoking so he would stop coughing and encouraged him to take up yoga to manage his short temper. She also got him to become a pescatarian, eating only fish, fruit, and vegetables.

In just a few months, the Big Bad Wolf was no longer a coughing, angry mess, and his friends started calling him Billy again. The truth about the construction came out, but the old story lingered, and the video occasionally popped up on social media. Billy was a changed man, but he couldn't change what happened. All he could do was manage how he responded to his situations in the future.

From his father's terrible incident, Butch Wolf saw an opportunity to help businesses and individuals manage their reputations through active marketing. He tells his clients to be aware of what is said about them and their business (especially if it is negative) and how to respond to it carefully.

Butch coaches his clients to pay attention to their online reviews and reply to all of them, good or bad. He encourages his clients to post the positive reviews they receive on their websites and in their advertising to make potential customers more interested and comfortable about doing business with them. In addition, he uses press releases to promote good news about his clients' products and services and when they have special events like grand openings or when they win an award.

When it comes to social media, Butch's rule is that a post must be true and helpful to go on the internet. And if someone says something mean or untrue about one of his clients, he is ready to respond.

He may even encourage his client to make some personal changes for the better, as his dad did.

THINK ABOUT
REPUTATION MANAGEMENT

Two things are true. First, your reputation is your brand. (Billy's brand was a combination of his knowledge and skill as a building inspector AND being a grumpy chain-smoking mess.) Second, you can change your reputation. (Billy's brand retained his expertise, and he chose to upgrade his personal image.) Use these questions to understand your brand's current reputation and identify how to strengthen or maintain your good name.

- What would a potential client learn about you on the internet?

- What do colleagues and clients say about you in the marketplace?

- How can you improve or maintain your reputation?

PINOCCHIO

Geppetto was a woodcarver who made puppets and longed to have a son. One day, he created a puppet and named him Pinocchio. The Blue Fairy, knowing that Geppetto was a good man and would be a great dad, brought Pinocchio to life and told the puppet that if he was honest, after a while, he could be a real boy.

To ensure that he always told the truth, the Blue Fairy put a spell on Pinocchio's nose so it would grow longer any time he lied. It would also go back to standard size once he rectified his deceit.

It is tough for any child to stay on the straight and narrow, and for a puppet with very few brain cells, it was nearly impossible. Pinocchio ended up running with the wrong crowd, skipping school, getting kidnapped to a desert island and turned into a mule.

And just when it couldn't get worse, Geppetto who was attempting to rescue Pinocchio, got swallowed by a whale. Luckily, Pinocchio saved him by making the mammoth mammal sneeze, hurling the duo out of the whale's mouth, over the waves, and onto the beach.

When they were safely ashore, the Blue Fairy appeared and commended Pinocchio for his bravery and honesty. Then, much to Geppetto's joy, she turned Pinocchio into a real boy.

CHAPTER 9

HONESTLY, PINOCCHIO! – SALES SKILLS

When Pinocchio told the truth and became a real boy, he and his dad, Geppetto, expanded their toy store. Pinocchio was primarily responsible for helping customers select the best toy for each child, while Geppetto made the wooden toys and handled the bookkeeping. They worked very well together.

Pinocchio knew every gizmo, game, and book in the shop. He also knew what type of person would like a particular item and who wouldn't. His knowledge was a boon for his customers because they understood they could always find the perfect gift for their favorite child by enlisting Pinocchio's help. He would ask questions about the child, how old they were, what interested them, whether they were active or quiet, and other questions to match the most suitable toy to their needs.

One day, the sales representative from the Best Bicycle Company (BBC) stopped by the shop to see Geppetto. The rep offered him the chance to sell their new line of kids bicycles. At first, Geppetto thought it was a bad idea because no one in town owned a bike.

Then Pinocchio piped up and said that girls and boys in

other towns loved bikes and having them at their shop would be great.

However, there was one slight problem: Pinocchio had never had a bike or even knew how to ride one. The BBC sales rep offered to get him a bike and teach him how to ride. So, Geppetto and Pinocchio agreed they would take a test shipment of bicycles the next month.

It wasn't easy learning to ride a bike. Pinocchio started with training wheels and slowly built up his confidence and balance. He would cautiously ride around the little town, and all the kids would run over to see what he was doing. After a few weeks, he took the training wheels off and started down the road. He was okay for the first 30 seconds, but then he saw a bluebird which distracted him and he lost his balance. Fortunately, he fell on the grass and was wearing his helmet. He hopped back on, paid attention, and carefully rode his bike home just in time for dinner.

Pinocchio also learned how to be a bike mechanic to fix and maintain his bicycle. So, when the month was over, he knew almost as much about bikes as the BBC representative. (They had been having regular training calls, and the rep was available to answer questions for tricky repairs.)

When the first shipment of bicycles was delivered, kids lined up to see the display. Pinocchio was busier than ever, ensuring each child got a bike that fit them and their personality. He asked a series of questions just as he had when finding a suitable toy or game for them. Of course, Pinocchio made sure each rider purchased a properly-fitted helmet and he went even further by offering bike riding lessons and safety courses for new riders.

Geppetto was thrilled to see the business boom and was glad he and Pinocchio had taken the opportunity to learn about their new products. Because of his knowledge, customers trusted Pinocchio to help select the right bike for each child in town, and in just one year, he became the Best Bicycle Company's top salesperson!

THINK ABOUT
SALES SKILLS

If you have a business and want it to be successful, you must do sales. Sales is not marketing. Marketing is making people aware that you offer a solution. Sales is determining if your solution is the right one for your prospect. Use these questions to explore how you approach sales and identify how you might improve your process.

- How do you feel about sales and salespeople?

- What is your biggest challenge with being a sales professional?

- What products or services can you combine to better serve your customers and clients?

- Who can help you improve your sales skills?

THE BOY WHO CRIED WOLF

There once was a young shepherd who was afraid of the dark and got very lonesome sitting out in the fields with the sheep at night. His job was to watch the sheep and protect them from predators, but he wasn't sure who or what would protect him. The scared shepherd had a flashlight and his shepherd's crook, but whenever he heard a moth flutter or the wind sigh, he would freeze with terror.

While sitting on the hillside one night, he saw something creeping across the field. It swiveled its head in his direction, and two yellow eyes glared at him. Panicked, the shepherd jumped up and screamed, "WOLF! WOLF! WOLF!"

The townspeople heard the alarm and came running up the hill, armed to defeat the wolf. Meanwhile, the critter ran right by the startled shepherd. It was his neighbor's cat. When the townspeople arrived, the shepherd explained that he had made a mistake and apologized for his error. Since he was new to the job, the townspeople agreed it could happen to anyone, and they ambled back to their homes.

The next night, the shepherd was bundled up, sitting against a tree, when a near-frozen snake sought the warmth of his blanket. The shepherd felt the slithery visitor and bolted to his feet, screeching, "WOLF! WOLF! WOLF!"

Again, the townspeople rushed to the meadow, ready

to take on the wolf, but there was none. This time, the embarrassed shepherd invented a great story about the size and ferocity of the non-existent beast and how he fended it off with his crook while the townspeople were still pulling on their boots. They seemed to accept his tale but grumbled about it all the way home.

On the third night, the creature the shepherd had invented actually showed up. The shepherd cried out, "WOLF! WOLF! WOLF!" But this time, no one believed him. They all stayed home until the next morning and then saw their sheep were gone.

CHAPTER 10

THE BOY WHO CRIED SALE! – IT'S NOT ABOUT THE PRICE.

Marcus Slot's uncle had built a reputation for having a pristine shoe shop with a great selection, excellent service, and fair prices. However, Marcus believed that what customers truly desired was a deal. After all, the store flooded with customers during the end-of-season sales, so his thinking was that by offering sale prices all the time, your store would always be busy.

With that idea in mind, Marcus quit working at his uncle's store in the city and rolled into town to open The Shoe Cellar, a store with everything from baby shoes to work boots at deep discounts.

All of Marcus' marketing announced that he had the best shoes at exceptionally reduced prices, which made customers very interested in visiting his shop. The Shoe Cellar ads featured pictures of designer stilettos, name-brand sneakers, and sturdy hiking boots right below a headline that announced, "DISCOUNT PRICES!" Above his storefront window, Marcus strung up a vivid yellow banner with 3-foot-high black letters screaming "SALE!"

When potential customers came into the shop, they were surprised to find one double-sided stack of shoeboxes running from the front door to the back of the store and the three surrounding walls stuffed to the ceiling with beat-up shoeboxes. There was no system for identifying the size or style of the shoes except by reading the occasionally mislabeled carton.

Most people were not willing to search through the disarray to retrieve their bargains, but those who did were pleased with their find and the price. However, after a few months, Marcus noticed he didn't have many repeat customers, so he tried another tactic. He announced that the store would close for remodeling and that there would be a grand re-opening sale.

When the store was ready, Marcus strung up his old "SALE!" banner with "GRAND RE-OPENING" added. Inside The Shoe Cellar, the boxes were now in order by size and style, and the shoes' prices remained discounted. Now, when a customer wanted a particular pair of shoes, Marcus would retrieve the box and assist the customer. Then, at checkout, he added an upcharge for his service on top of the price of the shoes.

Initially, customers were stunned by such a brazen policy. Most were either too enamored with their find or too proud to look cheap and paid the service fee without complaint. Others left their shoes at the counter and stormed out of the shop, vowing to tell their friends they had been misled. Again, after a few months (being a slow learner), Marcus realized he still didn't have many repeat customers.

He decided to give it one last shot. He remade his big yellow banner to read, "PREMIUM SERVICE & SALE PRICES!" He changed his marketing to show people that he included his superior customer service with the deeply discounted prices. And then he waited.

One or two people stopped in, mostly out of curiosity, but by then no one believed The Shoe Cellar was the ideal place to buy their next pair of shoes. Finally, in desperation, Marcus called his uncle to ask for his old job back and to try to understand what went wrong.

"People come to my store because they trust me to provide consistent quality in both my service and my products," his uncle said. "Of course, the store is busier when I have a sale. The regular customers and occasional shoppers are looking for a bargain and the opportunity to brag about getting it from my store."

"It's quite simple," his uncle stated, "People buy what they value."

THINK ABOUT

IT'S NOT ABOUT PRICE

Products and services are not priced for what they are but for what they deliver. For instance, you can pick up a pair of flip-flops for a couple of bucks at just about any store in the summertime. However, those identical flip-flops will be more valuable and more expensive when you need to buy them at a Caribbean resort in February. Use these questions to better understand the value you bring to the marketplace to avoid selling yourself short.

- What is the difference between your value and your price?

- How do you present your value to potential customers?

- What do your current customers value about working with you?

- What additional value can you add to your products or services?

CITY MOUSE & COUNTRY MOUSE

The City Mouse visited her good friend, the Country Mouse, and was appalled at her lifestyle. First, the Country Mouse lived in a barn, and her floors were strewn with straw. For lunch, she served some grains she'd gathered from the horse trough and a tiny bit of cheese she had stolen from the kitchen. There was no tea to drink; they sipped only rainwater.

It would have been impolite for the City Mouse to point out her friend's meager circumstances, so instead, she invited her to come to the city and enjoy the luxury of her home.

When they arrived, Country Mouse was overwhelmed by the posh surroundings. The rugs under her feet were softer than clouds, and the fireplace kept everything very snug. When it was time for dinner, the pair scampered into the kitchen and up onto the counter. There, they found platters of cheese, a loaf of dark bread, a bowl of grapes, and a cookie jar.

As they were about to dive into the cookie jar, the hostess let out a terrified squeak! The house cat had stalked them and was ready to pounce. The mice bounded off the counter and dashed into the mousehole by the stove with the cat hot on their tails.

Breathless, the Country Mouse said, "You are in grave danger! You must leave at once!"

The City Mouse said, "Oh, no. I always outsmart the beast."

The Country Mouse shook her head and said, "I have no tolerance for terror. I am going home to my simple place filled with peace."

She left immediately, and when she arrived home, she thought her humble abode never looked so wonderful.

CHAPTER 11

STADT & DORF – COMPETITION

Mr. Martin Dorf was the guy everyone in the village went to for car repairs. Dorf Auto Service was a small shop with two service bays and two mechanics who worked with Dorf. He and his team lived in the village and knew just about every single person, what kind of car they drove, who their kids were, and how their grandmas were doing. They were consistently busy but also found a way to help whomever they could when something unexpected came up.

Mr. Hugo Stadt, a well-dressed businessman trying to return to the city after spending a weekend in the countryside, limped into town on a flat tire. Dorf, of course, fixed the flat, and Mr. Stadt was back on the road home to his high rise in no time.

A week later, Stadt returned to tell Dorf he would put him out of business. He stated, "I am bringing my franchised car repair service to town, and you can either join me or plan to close up your shop."

Dorf said, "We'll see."

Word got out that another garage would soon be opening, and the locals started hypothesizing the outcome. Some said the competition was good, but they would not switch from Dorf.

Others said it would depend on the price—if Stadt was less expensive, then there would be no other choice but to get their car serviced there. Some spoke about loyalty to Dorf, but Stadt's new technology countered that argument. The town was in quite an uproar.

In no time at all, Big Stadt Car Service opened its sparkling new garage. They ordered coffee and donuts. A smiling receptionist greeted everyone and six mechanics stood ready in pristine uniforms. The latest gizmos and gadgets filled the shop. They could maintain and repair your car with ease, and a small showroom displayed shiny accessories for every vehicle.

On the very first day, Mr. Dorf walked over and congratulated Mr. Stadt on his new venture. With a cocky smile, Stadt said, "Thanks, but be aware. I meant what I said. I will be putting you out of business." Dorf grinned, gave a little shrug, and replied, "We'll see."

Stadt's first attempt at shuttering Dorf was offering an oil change for 20 percent less. Then he tried windshield wiper replacement, also at a deep discount. Finally, he had a tire sale—buy one, get three free! Naturally, customers lined up at Big Stadt's to snag the deals, but most went back to Dorf's little shop for other maintenance or repair issues.

After a year, Big Stadt Car Service was floundering, while Dorf Auto Service continued doing business as usual, only slightly impacted by the competition. Meanwhile, Mr. Stadt was losing money. But he was so committed to shutting down the competition that he didn't care. He kept the repair shop open with the profits from his other locations.

One day, Mr. Dorf invited Mr. Stadt to lunch to talk about business. Stadt was skeptical about the friendly invitation and a little embarrassed but agreed to meet. After they got through the stilted hellos and how-are-yous, Dorf said, "I imagine this is awkward for you since you planned to put me out of business.

Fortunately for me, you haven't succeeded. I can reveal why you failed, and then, if you are interested, I'll tell you how we can succeed ... together." Stadt replied that he was eager to listen and learn.

Dorf explained that he was committed to his community. He and his business supported charitable causes like the food bank, sponsored sports programs for kids, and volunteered for all sorts of things to help enhance the community. By being involved in so many positive activities, the folks in the village got to know, like, and trust him. He also knew the best problem-solvers in town, meaning other merchants and service providers, from dog walkers and babysitters to dentists and veterinarians. He was a trusted resource for people seeking solutions.

"Each of us has our Circle of Influence. It may be the people you regularly meet for coffee, the parents of the soccer team you coach, or your business networking group." Dorf continued, "These people know you as a person, not just as somebody trying to sell them something. They see the quality of your character.

That's why this town trusts me to service their cars. They know me, and I know them."

Stadt was stunned that Dorf would share his secret for success. He also thought it sounded like a lot of work. Dorf shook his head. "Getting to know people and understanding what they need to have a good life is not work; it's being human. And it makes your life better, too!"

Next, Dorf said, "You have top-shelf mechanics as I do, but you also have technology that I don't. I would like to send people to your shop when we can't fit them in or have a problem we can't seem to solve. You see, there is enough business here for both of us. And," he added with a wink, "you've got that neat accessory shop that I think will do very well once people get to know you."

Dorf and Stadt smiled, shook hands, ordered lunch, and got down to talking about the things they loved most, cars and their families, but maybe not in that order.

THINK ABOUT

COMPETITION

Knowing your competition is a great way to expand your industry knowledge, better define your marketplace, and stay invested in your success. Use these questions to better understand your competition and their differences and similarities.

- Who is your competition?

- What do they do that you don't?

- How could you work together?

THE TORTOISE AND THE HARE

The Tortoise was out for her morning stroll when she ambled past the Hare. "Could you possibly go any slower?" the Hare asked ruefully. The Tortoise, ignoring the attitude, replied, "No, I don't believe I could."

Nearby, the folks gathered outside the coffee shop giggled and agreed that going any slower would most likely mean standing still. The Hare loved having an audience, so she hopped in front of the Tortoise and said, "Let's race!" The crowd gasped.

The Tortoise said, "Sure! When?"

"Now," hissed the Hare.

The Badger held up a white flag as the contestants approached the starting line. He dropped the flag, and the Hare bounded off, covering the first third of the course in two hops.

The Tortoise pointed her nose at the finish line and carefully put one foot in front of the other. Far up ahead, the Hare decided to take a little nap while the Tortoise caught up.

The Hare awoke when she heard the crowd cheering for the Tortoise. Incredibly, she had just passed the Hare and had now taken the lead. The Hare jumped up and bounced past the Tortoise, stopping a few feet from the finish line. Then she opened her backpack and pulled out a snack. "Gee, all that work made me kind of hungry," the snarky Hare said. "I think I'll have a bite while I wait for the Tortoise."

Step by step, the Tortoise plodded her way to where the Hare was sitting and again passed her. The crowd went wild, cheering her on. The Hare relaxed against a tree finishing her last bite of carrot cake, knowing she could leap to the finish line and beat the Tortoise in a heartbeat.

When the Hare finally decided to get back in the race, the Tortoise's nose was inches from the victory ribbon. The Hare stood up to make the great leap and claim the victory, but instead, she got tangled in her backpack straps and tumbled into a heap. The Tortoise, grinning slightly, slowly and steadily crossed the finish line, winning the race as the crowd roared for her success.

CHAPTER 12

CONSISTENT EFFORT WINS THE RACE – MARKETING PLANS

Shelly Tortuga and Esther Lepus were friendly competitors and business partners as owners of the two Coffee Corner shops. These identical coffee spots were on the east and west corners of Main Street to catch people on their way in and out of town. Shelly ran the one on the west side of the street, and Esther had the east side.

Everything about the stores was precisely the same. The partners believed in maintaining the same rules and protocols for their team, offered identical products, and kept the same hours. The only difference was the manager and how they marketed the cafés.

At their Thursday business meeting, Shelly and Esther talked about marketing. They had exactly the same budget and other resources, but each had their own way of keeping the shop top of mind with their customers.

Shelly was committed to a consistent content marketing schedule. Her plan included a weekly email announcing the special of the week, a twice-weekly blog about community events, and a cheerful post on social media at 5:30 every morning to brighten the day. (Her customer count was consistently growing.)

Esther's marketing plan was very different. She would sporadically reach out to her customers, usually with a flurry of activity for a week or two, get overwhelmed, and stop for a month or more before going at it again. (Her customer count always jumped when she paid attention to her marketing and then slumped again when she stopped.)

Esther said her way was best because she had lots of time to rest and develop new ideas before jumping back into the promotions. Shelly quietly stated that her system was better because it was very orderly and structured. "Wanna bet?" asked Esther.

With that challenge, the two owners set a goal of selling 5,000 cups of RUN FOR GOLD coffee in 30 days, and whoever got there first was the winner of the Golden Coffee Mug and bragging rights. They agreed to hang a RUN FOR GOLD coffee cup poster in each of their storefront windows announcing the upcoming competition and that they would award $5,000 to the local food bank at the end of the race. The 5K cup race was to start on Monday, so they each had only a few days to put their plans in place. They shook hands and started to prepare.

Esther immediately got busy planning her marketing strategy. She frantically wrote content for blogs, took pictures to post, created email newsletters, and made flyers for the store. As usual, Shelly calmly created the needed content and consistently posted as she always had.

During the first week, Esther took the lead as she had plastered news of the race (and instructions to go to Coffee Corner East) everywhere she could think of, including on the lampposts on her side of the street. By the end of the week, she was ahead of Shelly by 400 cups of coffee, which was a huge lead.

The second week, Shelly caught up to Esther by doing nothing more than her usual media. Meanwhile, Esther had to remove her posters from the lamp posts because they were considered an eyesore. The time she could have spent on her marketing campaign had to be used instead for taking down posters and peeling the tape off the lamp posts.

By the end of the third week, Shelly passed Esther, and Coffee Corner West was only 400 cups away from the 5,000-cup finish line. Esther was lagging behind by almost 700 cups. Still confident that she could make up the difference, Esther ignored her previous marketing plan to try something new.

Esther was a guest on Little Boy Blue's local events podcast. During the interview, Esther encouraged people to support the RUN FOR GOLD race and the food bank. Being on the podcast was a great idea, but the listeners couldn't tell Coffee Corner East from West, and combined with Shelly's regular marketing, the podcast boosted her over the top in just 28 days.

The local media was there when Esther awarded Shelly the Golden Coffee Cup. As they presented the food bank with the $5,000 check and posed for pictures, Esther hollered, "I'll win the rematch! Shelly was just lucky." Shelly smiled, knowing it wasn't luck; it was her consistent effort that won the race.

THINK ABOUT
MARKETING PLANS

As in the original fable, Shelly kept her focus on the goal, and while it wasn't glamorous or exciting, her consistent effort made her successful. Use these questions to explore your current marketing plan and determine what you are willing to do consistently to ensure your success.

- What type of marketer are you - sporadic, consistent, or non-existent?

- How do you attract new customers?

- How do you connect with your existing customers?

- What would you change about your current marketing plan?

- Who can help you make those changes?

THE RED SHOES

There was nothing that Giselle loved more than to dance. One day, she passed the shoemaker's, spied a pair of ruby-red satin ballet slippers, and found the second thing she could love. She immediately went into the shop and asked to purchase the shoes.

The shoemaker explained that the shoes were not for sale but only for display because, unfortunately, they were enchanted; whoever wore them would never stop dancing.

That made Giselle want the shoes all the more. For hours, she begged the shoemaker to sell her the shoes, and weary of her pleading, he agreed to sell them to her at an outrageous price that he thought Giselle would never pay. Downhearted at the cost but still determined to purchase the red shoes, she said, "I will be back for those shoes. They are meant to be mine!"

Months passed, and every day, Giselle stopped by the shop window to gaze at the red shoes. She worked constantly and slept very little, saving every penny to purchase them. After nearly a year, she entered the shop to buy her heart's desire.

The shoemaker warned her again that the red shoes were cursed and dangerous. He encouraged her to spend her money elsewhere, but all Giselle wanted was the shoes and to dance. She would not be dissuaded.

Finally, the shoemaker sold her the shoes. Giselle gleefully paid for her purchase and sat on a stool to lace and tie the beautiful ruby red shoes. She rose up on her toes, her face radiant with joy, and started to dance. Giselle danced in the shop, then out to the street, and into the countryside, never to be seen again.

CHAPTER 13

THE RED SHOE BALLET SCHOOL – BALANCE

Giselle was born to dance, and her parents signed her up for ballet lessons when she was just three years old. Being a slightly shy person, Giselle took Fritz, her fluffy white, floppy-eared stuffed dog, with her to the first dance class for moral support. He was a gift from her godmother, Wendy.

Fritz was her best and constant audience. His big brown button eyes watched over her as she learned to do barre work and attempted the ballet positions. The rest of the class enjoyed having Fritz as their guardian, so Giselle brought him with her every week.

Giselle won the coveted Red Shoes Scholarship in high school and attended the New York School of Ballet. Fritz lived in her dorm room while she was at college, not allowed to attend her classes, but still able to keep a watchful eye on her.

After graduation, she joined the Alvin Ailey American Dance Theater, started teaching the youngest dancers, and brought Fritz back into the studio. He comforted the little kids who would give him hugs and tell him secrets, like when they were anxious about performing.

While Giselle loved being in New York City and teaching the children, she was homesick and wanted to be near her family and friends. She returned home and rented a storefront to create her Red Shoe Ballet School.

Being very independent, Giselle did almost all the work of transforming the store into a school herself, even refusing to accept help from friends and family. When she opened the doors, students flooded in, ready to learn.

Giselle taught the classes, planned the performances, made the costumes and the sets, maintained the school, and handled all the business issues from registrations to rent. She was utterly devoted to her business, and it was going well. Fritz was still beside her, plopped on a shelf near her desk, looking rather forlorn.

Fritz was as worried as a stuffed puppy could be. He could see that she was still missing her family and friends even though she was now just minutes away from all of them. She frequently turned down their offers to take a stroll, go on a picnic, or come for dinner. Her answer was always some variation of, "Sorry, I have to work!"

Even on her birthday, Giselle was at the ballet school. Since it was Sunday and the school was closed, she was startled when her Godmother rapped on the door. Wendy announced: "You work too much; you are out of balance. You need to see the sky and the people who love you. Let me introduce you to Harmonia!" Tucked under Wendy's arm was a little dog that looked just like Fritz, but this one was real!

Giselle was accustomed to Wendy speaking directly and with love. She scooped Harmonia out of Wendy's arms, and the puppy immediately snuggled up and started licking Giselle's face. "Let's make a plan!" said Wendy.

"First of all, you must know there is nothing wrong with asking for help," Wendy announced. She then explained that while Giselle was a woman of many talents, she could benefit from the wisdom, knowledge, and skills that other colleagues and cohorts had to offer. By tapping into those resources, Giselle could focus on the areas of her passion and expertise while continuing to build her business and regain her personal balance.

As Harmonia napped on her blanket, with Fritz happily keeping her company, Giselle and Wendy created a new strategy for running the school, including hiring a cleaning company, a virtual assistant, and a bookkeeper. They even plotted how to get parent volunteers to help with costuming, set building, and publicity.

By turning over specific tasks to professionals and accepting help from knowledgeable volunteers, Giselle had free time for daily walks with Harmonia and frequent visits with loved ones. And that meant The Red Shoe Ballet School could still flourish, and so would Giselle.

THINK ABOUT
KEEPING YOUR BALANCE

Being an entrepreneur can be all-consuming, especially when you start your business and when you grow it, whether it's doing well or not so great. However, there are ways to maintain your sense of humor, your health, and your loving relationships without the business completely consuming you. Use these questions to take a quick assessment of your current balance status.

- How well are you able to keep your health, business, and relationships in balance?

- Which of these three areas needs more attention? What changes can you make to improve your balance? Who or what can help you?

GOLDILOCKS & THE THREE BEARS

Goldilocks liked to wander the woods on her own, and one day, she happened upon a cozy little cottage. It was late morning; she felt peckish and thought she might ask for some refreshment. She knocked on the door wearing her best smile, ready to charm whoever answered. When there was no answer, she brazenly opened the door, hollered, "Hello?", and walked in.

Inside, she found a tidy home with three chairs that were obviously sized for the occupants. She tested each one. One was too large, another too small (which promptly broke when she sat in it), but the third was just right.

After sitting for what she felt was a polite amount of time, she approached the kitchen table set for breakfast with three bowls of porridge. She tested each one. One was too hot, one was too cold, but the last one was just right, and she devoured it.

The porridge made her dozy. Goldilocks slipped down from her chair and looked for a place to nap. She found three beds in the bedrooms, tested them all to find the one that was just right, and went quickly to sleep.

Minutes later, the residents of the home returned. Momma, Papa, and Baby Bear snuffled around, unhappy, finding a chair broken, some of their porridge eaten, and a stranger in Baby's bed. Their growls startled Goldilocks out of her slumber, and she dashed out the door, deciding to only enter other people's homes when invited.

CHAPTER 14

BEARISH GOLDILOCKS – PROSPECT SELECTION

Goldilocks ran *Just Right*, her well-established interior design firm. She focused on making homes livable and functional for the inhabitants. One of her crowning achievements was revamping the home for the woman living in a shoe with her large brood. It was a pro-bono assignment that Goldilocks took on since many of those kids were in school with her own children.

The local media covered the unveiling of the rehabbed home, and suddenly, Goldilocks had more prospective clients than she could reasonably handle. She quickly had to figure out how to choose whom to work with, so she came up with her criteria.

First – They needed a workable budget and be willing to pay a deposit to get started.

Second – They must be flexible and have a reasonable time frame for the work to be completed.

Third – They must have a compatible personality and be respectful to her and her team.

Goldilocks was satisfied that these three criteria would help her clearly identify her ideal client. Next, she developed a three-step process to weed out inappropriate prospects. Step One: she'd have an initial meeting at her office to learn about the person, their budget, and their goals.

Once she felt they were a good fit, she would go to Step Two and perform a site survey to confirm the client's expectations. And finally, in Step Three, she would schedule another meeting at her office to confirm everything, review the contract, and secure the deposit. While this process would be an investment of her time, she felt it was worth it to avoid problems and regret down the road.

To start the process with her three top prospects, she sent them each an invitation to work with her. In her message, Goldilocks explained her 3-step process and concluded the invitation with, "I believe in working with my clients to create the home environment they desire. We will be on this journey together, so it is important to determine if we can be good partners." All three agreed to start the process, and Goldilocks prepared to use her criteria.

Ms. Ursula Minor arrived 15 minutes late to the appointment with no apology or explanation. Ms. Minor reeked of money, was an upstanding member of the community (very well connected, don't you know), and felt that Goldilocks' process was totally unnecessary. Ms. Minor expected to blurt out her design ideas for her new kitchen, drop a deposit for half the cost, and book the start date.

Goldilocks could barely get a word in with Ms. Minor but finally said, "I'm sorry, that is not my process, and I don't feel I can serve you properly. Thank you for coming to meet with me today, and I hope you find another designer who will be a better partner for you." Ms. Minor left in a huff. Goldilocks poured a chamomile tea and prepared for her next prospect, Mrs. Carry Pauvre.

Mrs. Pauvre arrived right on time, was very cheerful, and was just a bit anxious about meeting with Goldilocks. It was Mrs. Pauvre's first time working with an interior designer, as she had always done her own remodeling and decoration. However, she had just inherited a considerable sum and thought it would be nice to splurge and hire a professional team.

That initial meeting went so well that Goldilocks and Mrs. Pauvre immediately scheduled the site survey for the next day. On-site, Mrs. Pauvre was again pleasant, easy to work with, clear about her expectations, and flexible about her timeline for her first-floor update. That evening, Goldilocks created a plan and prepared for the contract review appointment scheduled for the next afternoon.

Mrs. Pauvre was again punctual and still pleasant but teary-eyed. She thanked Goldilocks profusely for her time and expertise while explaining that she could not hire *Just Right* for the job. Her spouse had felt that the expense was indulgent and that the remodeling would have to wait until their two children, a freshman and a junior in college, graduated. Goldilocks was disappointed but wished Mrs. Pauvre the best and looked forward to seeing her around town.

Mr. Levar Clase arrived a few minutes later and just a bit early for his appointment. He came prepared with a vision board for his new music room. After a few moments, Mr. Clase quietly said, "As an accountant, I maintain a very professional demeanor. However, when I am at home, I wish to have a place to listen to music and play my piano as loudly as I like, but without bothering the neighbors."

He had already estimated the cost for the elements of his renovation and built his budget with a substantial cushion for unforeseen expenditures. Goldilocks was cautiously excited to book the site survey with Mr. Clase.

The site survey went smoothly, and as soon as Goldilocks announced she had the plan ready, Mr. Clase requested the earliest possible appointment to review the contract and schedule the job. At that meeting, Goldilocks and Mr. Clase agreed to the budget, the timetable, the preferred communication method, and the amount of the down payment.

They signed the contract, shook hands, and both felt that this partnership was just right.

THINK ABOUT
PROSPECT SELECTION

Your business is not for everyone. Only a select few need, want, and are willing to pay for the products and services you offer. Among those folks are the people who you would enjoy working with. Use these questions to define a process for turning prospects into clients you'd like to work with.

- How do you currently select your prospects?

- What is your process for agreeing to work with a prospective client?

- How and when do you turn down a prospect?

- What changes will you make in your selection process?

THE UGLY DUCKLING

A duck had just hatched her clutch of five eggs, and as she inspected each chick, she recognized that one was larger than the others and grey instead of yellow. Still, she was proud of her brood and took them to the pond to show them off.

The other fowl started whispering behind their wings that the grey one was the ugliest duckling they had ever seen. Mother Duck ignored them and encouraged her little family to do the same.

As the ducklings grew, four got their lovely duck feathers, while the large grey one was a molting mess of down and dull beige. Even his siblings started to say he was ugly. Heartbroken, the Ugly Duckling slipped off one night to the other side of the pond to fend for himself.

Mother Duck spent weeks searching for him and never found her Ugly Duckling. Just as she was about to give up, she paddled up to a handsome swan and said, "I am searching for my son. He was not the prettiest duck, but he has the best heart, and I miss him terribly."

The swan said, "Mother! I am your ugly duckling! And I have missed you, too!" Together, the duck and the swan swam back to join the rest of their family, and no one called him ugly again.

Except for his brother, as a term of endearment because that's what siblings do.

CHAPTER 15

THE UGLY DUCKLING –
CONSIDERING ALTERNATIVES

The Eider family had been making pillows for over 50 years. Grampa Eider had started the business with his seven children, tending the flocks of ducks and following behind the birds to collect their fallen feathers. (Mr. Eider was very concerned about animal welfare.)

His seven children each had seven children, and all his sons worked at the Eider Down Pillow Factory. Over the years, the factory expanded its products beyond its world-famous pillows to include down-filled blankets and clothing. The business was doing very well, and it looked like the grandkids would all follow suit to work in the family business, except for his youngest grandson, Sven, who was allergic to feathers.

As a child, he had always been a scrawny boy with a runny nose and dark circles under his eyes. It wasn't until Sven went away to an engineering school that he realized it was the feathers that were making him miserable. He tossed his down pillow and stuffed his pillowcase with wool fleece instead. It was pretty comfortable, plus Sven stopped sneezing and slept much better.

When he came home on winter break just a few months

before graduation, he was no longer a runny-nosed, rangy little kid. He was now a healthy, confident young man dressed in a navy pea coat.

The changes in Sven caused quite a bit of grumbling within the family. Some of Sven's cousins made fun of him for wearing a wool coat rather than a down jacket. His brothers were disgusted with him for having wool blankets on his bed instead of a down comforter. His father just couldn't see a future in making pillows stuffed with wool and feared Sven would be unemployable.

However, Sven's mother wasn't as concerned. She imagined that there must be other people like Sven who were allergic to feathers and still needed pillows! She pulled Sven aside and suggested he look into non-allergenic materials to stuff pillows, comforters, and even clothing.

Sure enough, he came up with multiple alternatives. He was ecstatic! He learned that these products were readily available, some were natural, and others were made from recycled materials, which would appeal to customers who were down adverse.

As part of his research, Sven reached out to the owner of The Stuffing Factory outside of Boston, which created most of the alternative fillings. Stephanie Stuffing was delighted to hear from a member of the renowned Eider family, so she set up a video chat.

Like Sven, Stephanie was part of a family business and understood how boxed in people can get in their thinking. They spent a quick hour comparing notes about infrastructure, management, marketing, and product development. As the call wrapped up, Stephanie said, "Sven, I want you to think about coming to work for us. We could certainly use your expertise."

Sven blushed. He realized taking that job in Boston would be an excellent opportunity for him. "Thanks, Stephanie," he stammered. "I appreciate the offer and will sincerely consider it, but first, I want to see if I can do something here that will benefit both companies."

Over the next few days, Sven worked out all the details of expanding the Eider product line to include down-alternative products. He expected that his father and his uncles would be less than receptive to these new ideas, but he also felt that he had the numbers to prove the profitability.

Sven's grandfather always had a soft spot for the odd duck, so when Sven asked for a business meeting with him, Grampa Eider readily agreed. Through the grapevine, he had heard that Sven was talking with Stephanie Stuffing (always know what your competition is up to) and was worried that he may have decided to leave the family business.

As he entered the oak-paneled office, Sven sneezed. Duck down and feathers were everywhere in the building; luckily, Sven remembered to bring his inhaler in case his allergies got out of control. Wisely, his grandfather suggested they take their meeting outside to the snow-covered duck pond, hoping the fresh winter air would make Sven more comfortable.

Together, the two sat on the bench by the pond under a bright blue sky and talked about alternatives. Then, just as the sun was setting and their feet were almost numb, they walked back to the factory. On the way, Mr. Eider texted his sons to meet them at the front door so that he could give them the news.

Everyone was assembled, wrapped in their hooded down parkas and wearing their down mittens, anxious to hear what Mr. Eider had to say. "Boys, it's time for us to make some changes. We must look at alternatives, and Sven will lead the way!"

Shortly after Sven graduated, Grandfather built the new alternative factory next door and was ready to start production without a feather in sight. Now, that was nothing to sneeze at.

THINK ABOUT
CONSIDERING ALTERNATIVES

Whatever your product or service, innovations are always available that may help you do business better. It is up to you to pay attention to opportunities that might initially seem daunting but could improve what you offer. These innovations may be the tools or processes you use or the solutions you offer. Use these questions to review your feelings about potential alternatives and innovations in your industry.

- How do you respond to, "That's the way we've always done it?"

- What alternatives are available that might innovate your business?

- Who can help you find and implement these innovative alternatives?

CINDERELLA

Cinderella served her stepmother and two awful stepsisters as their housekeeper, cook, and maid. Her life was quite miserable as she could do nothing but take care of their needs and the household.

One day, an invitation to Prince Charming's Ball arrived. It said that all the single ladies should attend (with their chaperones) so that the Prince might find his true love. Cinderella thought this might be her chance to escape and was excited to go to the ball.

However, Cinderella's stepmother would not allow it, and on the night of the ball, she and the awful stepsisters left Cinderella sobbing by the fireside.

Once she'd had a good cry, Cinderella pulled herself together and started cleaning up. As she swept, an ember popped from the fire, landed on the hearth, and turned into a fairy. She introduced herself as Cinderella's Fairy Godmother and said she was there to ensure Cinderella got to the ball.

With a swoosh of her wand, the Fairy Godmother dressed Cinderella in the most beautiful gown, complete with the traditional uncomfortable shoes, which happened to be glass slippers. Then she plopped the maiden into a magical carriage and told her to be home before midnight, when the spell would expire.

As expected, Cinderella caught the eye of the Prince and danced with him until she heard the clock start to strike midnight. She dashed out of the palace, lost a slipper, and was back to her old ashy self on the twelfth bong of the clock.

The next day, the Prince set out to find the owner of the glass slipper. His last stop was Cinderella's home. The nasty sisters tried the slipper, but neither of the dreadful duo could get even their bunions into the shoe. As he was about to leave, the Prince spied a messy maiden in the shadows by the fireside. Figuring he had nothing to lose, he tried the slipper on Cinderella, and it fit!

After some introductions and negotiations, Cinderella and the Prince were married and lived as happily ever after as they could.

CHAPTER 16

CINDERELLA'S SOLUTIONS – SHARING EXPERTISE

Cinderella Charming was bored. She and Prince Charming had been married for a few years and lived happily, but she had very little to do now that she was a princess. To keep herself occupied between the fancy dress balls and fundraisers, she started documenting her cleaning methods from all her years of caring for her nasty stepmother and stepsisters.

Once she got her methods all in order, she again began to feel useless. When she mentioned it to her lady-in-waiting, Matilda, the Lady suggested that the Princess ask the cleaning staff to test her cleaning solutions and try her methods. The castle cleaning staff couldn't say, "No!" (Really, they couldn't.) And with feigned enthusiasm, they agreed to be Cinderella's beta test team.

Much to the castle crew's surprise and pleasure, her processes and potions truly worked. The castle never looked as sparkly as it did with Cinderella's eco-safe cleaning solutions and efficient methods. After a few days of feeling on top of the world, the Princess's lack of purpose started to sneak back in, and her mood once again became mopey.

Ever the ray of sunshine, Lady Matilda saw the darkness creeping up on the Princess and, in a sudden flash of insight, suggested Cinderella capture her cleaning wisdom in a book. Cinderella perked up at that idea and immediately fired up her tablet to create the book.

Along with her cleaning recipes and practices, she embellished the content with stories of her life before becoming Princess Charming.

Like most writers, she was compelled to come up with a title before starting in on the content and became a little petulant as she struggled to name her book. With a heavy sigh and a practiced smile, Lady Matilda gently offered, "What about *The Cinderella Solutions – How to clean happily ever after!?*" Cinderella sat straight up. "I love it! Perfect!" she proclaimed and proceeded to type away until summoned for dinner.

Weeks later, when she finished the first draft, Cinderella took it to Rapunzel to find out what it would take to turn her manuscript into a book. Her head was spinning when she learned that the words were not enough.

Rapunzel informed her Highness that she needed cover art, typography, editing, and marketing. It was more than Cinderella could possibly do on her own, not that she didn't have the time, but she lacked the expertise. The ever-wise Lady Matilda suggested that the Princess hire Rapunzel to edit her book, let the royal printer handle the artwork and typography, and have Butch Wolf manage her publicity and marketing.

In a few months, Cinderella had her book in hand, and Butch scheduled a meet-and-greet book signing at the local library. The conference room was overflowing with people anxious to learn from this royal cleaning expert. One of the attendees at the event came from the capital and owned a major home cleaning service.

He approached Lady Matilda to see if the Princess would be available to speak at their national convention.

Being a savvy person, Matilda set it up so that the Princess would appear at the convention via a video conference and donate her speaking fee to the library to upgrade their meeting rooms.

Matilda also negotiated that the fee would include the cost of printing two thousand books, which would be autographed by the author and given to each conference attendee.

After Cinderella spoke at the cleaning convention, she received multiple requests for other speaking opportunities, specifically training sessions. Matilda, recognizing that the Princess needed to tend to her royal duties, determined that online training would be the best way to reach the most people. Cinderella pre-recorded some sessions to maximize her efficiency, while others were presented live.

All those training sessions led to requests for Cinderella's products, which she hadn't yet created. So Matilda stepped in again and instructed (on behalf of the Princess) the royal engineer, architect, and chemist to develop a factory to produce the line of eco-friendly and sustainable cleaning solutions and tools. Then, she contacted the local labor board to find people to staff the factory and ship the products.

The book's success, training sessions, and products were a boon to the community. Cinderella used all the profits to support the local library, fund the food bank's organic garden, and provide the town with a pre-kindergarten. Her efforts (and Lady Matilda's) had a big payoff.

What started out of boredom as a simple book project became a flourishing business yielding local employment, quality products, and community support. Cinderella was no longer a bored princess but an empress of philanthropy.

THINK ABOUT
SHARING EXPERTISE

You are an expert in something. It may be your experience, the tools or techniques you use, or the benefits of your products and services. You can share your expertise through writing, speaking, and training opportunities. Use these questions to explore your expertise and how you might share it.

- Where does your expertise come from?

- How would you like to share your expertise?

- Who would you like to share your experience with?

- Who can help you take the next steps?

EPILOGUE

AND THEY LIVED HAPPILY EVER AFTER...

I know that because I wrote the endings to each of these stories. As an entrepreneur, you get to write your own success story, too.

From these little tales, I hope you learned that while you will encounter challenges as a small business owner, you can overcome them. Also, you are not alone on this adventure. You have a village of folks who really do want to see you succeed.

Of course, the voices that stand out to you the most are those of well-meaning friends and family who questioned your sanity the day you announced you were planning to start your own venture. Ignore them!

(Remember, in *Jack and the Beanstalk*, Jack's mother was not at all thrilled that he traded their scrawny cow for a handful of magic beans. Except for the run-in with the angry Giant, things turned out pretty well for them. They got a goose who laid golden eggs, a great passive income source. But that's another story.)

You have an idea that you want to see become a reality. You have the desire to bring something so special to the marketplace that you know people will need and want. It may be the tastiest Keto cookie, the most fabulous watercolor painting, or the best darn car wash. Your solutions and success will make your in-laws wonder why they ever doubted you.

Get out there and write your fairy tale with the mandatory happy ending. Your magic beans might be just what the market needs, even if they've never seen anything like them. Just be sure to tap into the resources in your area to guide you as you plan, build, and grow your business.

And please, if you have a minute, send me your story, then I can share it with other creative entrepreneurs so that they, too, can learn from you about living happily ever after.

Jane

Jane Maulucci

RESOURCES

I am slightly biased because I have the privilege of working with each of these authors. They generously share their wisdom through podcasts, blogs, and training sessions to help people succeed in their small business ventures. Each of them speaks from experience and from their heart. Read their books, glean their insights, and follow them for more business-building inspiration.

Riches in Niches: How to Make it BIG in a Small Market by Susan Friedmann

Relationship Marketing³: The Ground Game for Small Business Success by Martin Brossman

3 Circles Living by Todd Burrier

ACKNOWLEDGEMENTS

I've tried to make the point that even as a solopreneur, you never have to go it alone. While my name is listed as the author, I had a clever cohort who provided great input as I created the stories and lessons in this book.

Thank you to Heather Noto and Bonnie Chomica for their deep dive, thoughtful editing, and encouragement. It was painful, but I am so grateful! (Now I know how my clients feel!)

Thanks to my beta readers: Steven Sanders, Todd Burrier, Eileen Nonemaker, Deborah Kania, Barbra Carr, and Martin Brossman, who groaned at my humor and refined my content.

Thank you to Eileen Nonemaker for bringing Bo Peep's Calm Lamb to life as a very sweet logo and to Richard Grassi for creating my fabulous cover from my homely draft.

To Susan Friedmann and Bonnie Chomica, who listened patiently and laughed appropriately when I pitched the concept of this book in 2020, THANK YOU! They have been with me from the start, gently nudging and sometimes yanking me forward through the process. They are my Mastermind Team, and they make me smarter every time we talk!

Finally, thank you to the readers. May all your businesses flourish and your futures be happily ever after.

AFTERWORD

This book is more than pages and words. It is Jane's voice, her wisdom, and her heart living on. She poured herself into these ideas even when life made it hard. She believed they could help. That was Jane. She always showed up for others.

When Jane passed in September 2024, we lost a dear friend. We lost a brilliant colleague. We lost a light that made everything brighter. But she has not disappeared. She is here in every story. She is here in every piece of advice. She is here in every encouragement tucked into these chapters.

Her humor and wit are here too. You can feel it weaved through the stories. Jane had a way of making even the toughest lesson lighter with her quick turn of phrase. She had her own Jane-isms and a clever vocabulary that made us smile and sometimes laugh out loud. That spirit still shines in these pages.

This book came to life because of the love Jane inspired. Friends, family, and colleagues worked together to make sure it would be finished. We knew how much it mattered to her. We believed it could matter to you as well.

We miss her laughter. We miss her humor. We miss her Jane-isms and the sparkle in her words. We miss the way she could turn an ordinary moment into something unforgettable. Yet we are grateful that this book carries her spirit forward. Our hope is that as you turn the final page you feel Jane's presence too. She is cheering you on. She is reminding you of your own brilliance. She is nudging you to believe in what is possible.

Thank you, Jane, for your wit, your wisdom, and your heart. We carry you with us always.

Susan Friedmann
Founder & Owner, Aviva Publishing

100% of sales will be donated to charity

www.ingramcontent.com/pod-product-compliance
Lightning Source LLC
Chambersburg PA
CBHW030528210326
41597CB00013B/1070